YOUR KNOWLEDGE HAS VALUE

AF140268

- We will publish your bachelor's and
  master's thesis, essays and papers

- Your own eBook and book -
  sold worldwide in all relevant shops

- Earn money with each sale

Upload your text at www.GRIN.com
and publish for free

Bibliographic information published by the German National Library:

The German National Library lists this publication in the National Bibliography; detailed bibliographic data are available on the Internet at http://dnb.dnb.de .

Imprint:

Copyright © 2015 GRIN Verlag, Open Publishing GmbH
Print and binding: Books on Demand GmbH, Norderstedt Germany
ISBN: 978-3-668-20284-9

This book at GRIN:

http://www.grin.com/en/e-book/320397/the-concept-of-homo-economicus-and-experimental-games

Merve Gülacan

The concept of "Homo Economicus" and Experimental Games

Is "Homo Economicus" still alive today?

GRIN Publishing

GRIN - Your knowledge has value

Since its foundation in 1998, GRIN has specialized in publishing academic texts by students, college teachers and other academics as e-book and printed book. The website www.grin.com is an ideal platform for presenting term papers, final papers, scientific essays, dissertations and specialist books.

Visit us on the internet:

http://www.grin.com/

http://www.facebook.com/grincom

http://www.twitter.com/grin_com

IS *HOMO ECONOMICUS* STILL ALIVE?

Essay

Philosophy of Economics

Summer Term 2015

06.09.2015

CONTENTS

1. Introduction

"Traditional economic theory postulates an 'Economic Man', who, in the course of being 'economic' is also 'rational'. This man is assumed to have knowledge of the relevant aspects of his environment which, if not absolutely complete, is at least impressively clear and voluminous. He is assumed also to have a well-organized and stable system of preferences and a skill in computation that enables him to calculate, for the alternative courses of action that are available to him" (Simon, 1955, p. 99).

The findings of research in experimental behavioural economics over the past two decades have been impressively convincing. Until recently, economists assumed that individual behaviour is controlled by rationality. The consumer was perceived as a rational person who strives to maximize his utility. This is the concept of *homo economicus*, a prototype of an economic person and starting point for model formulation.However, this theory often overlooks the fact that *homo economicus* is not a person of flesh and blood, but a conceptual notion. Experimental evidence shows that the behaviour forecast by the standard model often does not correspond to reality. Factors like fairness, trust and moral values also play a role in the decision-making of the real economic actor. The knowledge gleaned from the observation of different negotiation plays provides the possibility for the derivation and representation of individual behaviour patterns. But the studies' findings reveal that feelings of fairness, generosity and trust play a crucial role for the results. The object of this work is to find an answer to the question if *homo economicus* is still alive or not. Therefore I will consider different experiments of the dictator game from the literature. Experimental games offer good possibilities for the representation and derivation of individual behaviour patterns.

Chapter 2 presents the concept of *homo economicus* and describes his properties. Chapter 3 deals with experimental games, with the major focus being on the dictator game. Individual studies will be presented. The last chapter concludes.

2. The concept of *Homo Economicus*

Until recently economists assumed that individual behaviour is controlled by rationality. *Homo economicus* acts exclusively in his own interest and strives for the maximization of his individual utility, which is usually understood as net economic gain. His preferences are constant and he has complete information. This is the concept of *homo economicus*, a prototype of an economic person and starting point for model formulation (Kirchgässner, 1991, p. 31). The last hundred years have seen some developments in and changes to this model of the "economic man", but all approaches still have a common core (Manstetten, 2000, p. 20). This basic concept of economic man is the starting point for a large part of the economic application models recognized today as well as for numerous experimental games. However, the model cannot represent all the characteristics of a real individual, but is a simplified representation of the typical actors seen in the economy. The ability to display fully rational behaviour is the main characteristic of *homo economicus*. He strives for utility maximization (this applies equally to consumers and producers and here refers to the special form of profit maximization). He is also continuously informed about all decision alternatives and their consequences. Thus, *homo economicus* acts as an objective function seeking to optimize wealth or income (Lofthouse and Vint, 1978, p. 586). The model of *homo economicus* can thus be regarded as a simplified model of the real man, which serves to explain certain social realities and human behaviours and their consequences (Tietzel, 1981, p. 118).

2.1 Properties of *Homo Economicus*

Due to the always present shortage of resources, an economic actor regularly finds himself facing decision situations which he must master in the best way possible. The standard model aims to serve as guidance for behaviour in such decision situations and therefore to better understand the economic actors. The characteristics of *homo economicus* are summarized below.

Rationality

Homo economicus makes his decisions rationally. He looks at all facets of a problem and weighs the advantages and disadvantages of possible solutions. He selects the solution that maximizes his own utility. Besides, he is ordinarily limited by restrictions in his scope of action. It should be noted that rational action is descriptive and not a normative demand within the scope of (economic) behavioural theory. In reality though, the two levels often merge, partly because one of the aims of economics is the ability to produce instructions for rational action (Tietzel, 1981, p. 120). Here rationality serves the empirical macroeconomic explanation of human action – regardless of whether that action is good or desired. In economics an actor acts rationally if he acts according to the economic principle: with the given resources, he reaches a maximum target, or achieves a given aim with a minimum of resources. Rational action thus is caused by shortages, here the shortage of the available resources. While this is clear enough, a second look at these central behavioural patterns of *homo economicus* is essential to be able to understand him as an explanatory model for economic methodology. In general one makes a distinction between two forms of rationality: formal and substantial rationality (Tietzel, 1981, p. 121f). Formal rationality refers to the way in which an actor makes decisions. A decision and the action following from it are rational when the actor has selected them systematically from the known action alternatives available to him. In formal rationality the logic and the consistency of all actions is tested. Such an examination is possible for an external observer if the present elements of the situation are known to him. Therefore nearly every action can be rational. The explanatory power of behaviour patterns and models becomes imprecise under consideration of all these factors, at least in the national economy theory. In this respect the action of *homo economicus* is not only formally but also substantially rational (Tietzel, 1981, p. 122).

Concepts like decisions, rationality etc. that play no role in the explanation pattern e.g. of physics are however central to the analysis of human action (Suchanek, 1994, p. 85f). Thereby it also becomes clear that the quality of *homo economicus* is to "act rationally".

Utility maximization

Utility maximization is the ultimate goal to which rational human action is directed. In this case, similarly to the rationality assumption, almost every action can be regarded as personal utility-maximizing – depending on the definition of the benefits, the objective function. In economic theory, profit maximization (or consumption) is usually used as the supreme "benefit" and hence the supreme or ultimate goal. In a biological approach, this would probably be the instinctive reproduction of one's own heritage.

The definition of the objective function is therefore dependent on the respective study subject. If reproduction is viewed from an economic perspective and if economic activities are examined through biological behaviour. Since the economic approach has its origins in the study of economic actions, selfishness is often equated with profit maximization. Actors use the resources available to them rationally to achieve this objective. In other words, the player behaves rationally if he maximizes his utility function under the given restrictions. He then achieves the maximum target value with the available resources or a given target with a minimum use of resources. He acts according to the economic principle. *Homo economicus* knows only economic goals and is motivated particularly by properties such as rational behavior, the pursuit of maximum benefit (utility maximization), the full knowledge of economic choices and their consequences, as well as complete information on all markets. *Homo economicus* is "neutral" to people; he is not concerned about whether the consequences of his actions are good or bad for other people. He looks at them neither with envy nor with malicious pleasure, nor does he take any pleasure in their well-being (Kirchgässner, 1991, p. 47). Nevertheless, the acceptance of utility maximization should not only be interpreted egoistically. But when actors cooperate, the disinterest understandably weakens – out of self-interest. Therefore, superficially disinterested action, or altruism, follows the self-interested logic of cooperative plays. To sum up, *homo economicus* acts in his environment and together with theirs to achieve his aims.

Self-interest

The prototype of the economic person incorporates no considerations about the well-being of others in his decision-making process. Only his own utility should be maximized. Whether others suffers is neither positively nor negatively valued except insofar as it results in a benefit or loss. If after the methodological individualism[1] the behaviour of the individuals taken together proves social action, this implies that the individuals act in their own interest and the self-interest axiom of the economic behavioural model is called:

---

[1] Methodological individualism: "[T]he socio-economic phenomenon under scrutiny is to be analysed by focusing on the individuals whose actions brought it about; understanding fully their 'workings' at the individual level; and, finally, synthesising the knowledge derived at the individual level in order to understand the complex social phenomenon at hand." (Varoufakis, Yanis, and Christian Arnsperger, 2006, p.7)

"The individual acts (only) according to his own interests and preferences" (Kirchgässner, 1991, p. 16). It is believed that people's behaviour is not influenced by the way of other people act.

Reaction to constraints

Changes in the behavior of *homo economicus* can be attributed to structural conditions. The environmental conditions provide the space for the actions of the actor, but on the other hand they limit him. The environmental conditions or restrictions include, for example: disposable income, the legal framework of action and the (expected) reactions of the other. Within the room for action lie the individual possibilities for action that are available the individual, and he can make a choice between them. This prevents focus on the restrictions that any behavioral change of the actors is attributed to changes in preferences. *Homo economicus* has one goal and it is to achieve his preference in the changing environment (Kirchgässner, 1991, p. 36f).

Constant preferences

It is generally assumed that the preferences of an economic man are constant, provided that the environmental conditions and restrictions do not change. One can therefore assume that an individual will always assess situations based on the same moral principles and therefore exhibit the same behaviour. The utility function and thus the preferences of *homo economicus* are assumed to be stable. Individual changes are usually ignored, also because they are relatively difficult to measure. In macroeconomic terms, the preferences may change in one person or in a group by changing the population structure. The restrictions or environmental conditions that govern the actions of individuals, however, are relatively easy to detect. If the changes in the ratios are determined, the items that are subject to the external conditions are kept identical in order to derive the various action sequences from the different situation conditions (Suchanek, 1994, p. 93).

Perfect information

Homo economicus is assumed to be perfectly informed about each alternative and its consequences. If the player responds to the restrictions in a certain way, then he fulfils the assumptions of *homo economicus*. He should pay no particular transaction and information costs, or "learning costs" (Soukup et al., 2014). He is fully aware of his alternatives, and he can assess the impact and consequences of the various alternatives. The adoption of full information results firstly from the rationality assumption. Rationality requires the actor's knowledge and predictability (up to foresight) of the possible consequences that will arise from each choice. Choosing the best alternative course of action can only be met in terms of its objective function. Secondly, the assumption of complete information is obviously an abstracting auxiliary assumption of economic methodology to analyse economic processes. Thus, *homo economicus* acts as an objective function seeking to optimize wealth or income (Lofthouse and Vint, 1978, p. 586).

2.2 Criticism

Although the concept of *homo economicus* plays an important role in the social sciences, there is hardly a concept that is so controversial. Even the above-described properties of *homo economicus* give rise to criticism and clearly show the limits of this model. The concept of *homo economicus* describes people as egoists. Of particular importance is how *homo economicus* actually performs in empirical research, which does not coincide with the model. These anomalies clearly put the model into question. It is indeed a general, but not a comprehensive model of human action that is variously useful in different fields of application (Kirchgässner, 2008, p. 202). The basic criticism focuses on the imputed "omniscience" and the "superhuman" abilities of *homo economicus*. Costs of information gathering and processing are ignored. In reality, perfect knowledge does not exist. Man is not a machine that has perfect information. In addition, the cognitive abilities of humans are limited and they make mistakes.

This is demonstrated by Kahneman and Tversky[2] and their studies on heuristics. Heuristics are simple rules which people often use to make decisions known or unknown. For example, anchoring[3] is a main heuristic. Heuristics show that people are not always aware

---

[2] "He was awarded the Nobel Prize in Economic Sciences in 2002 for his pioneering work integrating insights from psychological research into economic science, especially concerning human judgment and decision-making under uncertainty. Much of this work was carried out collaboratively with Amos Tversky" (http://kahneman.socialpsychology.org/, 05.09.2015).

[3] Anchoring: "During normal decision making, individuals anchor, or overly rely, on specific information or a specific value and then adjust to that value to account for other elements of the circumstance. Usually once the anchor is set, there is a bias toward that value" (http://www.sciencedaily.com/terms/anchoring.htm, 05.09.2015).

of their alternatives, and so cannot assess the impact and consequences of the various alternatives. There are so many points in the literature against the characteristics of *homo economicus*. The actors' thinking may be subject to fallacies. People align their actions to habits and internalized values and norms. In reality they often lack choices or information. At the same time, they decide according to past experience or expenses, relying on earlier cost-benefit calculations (Suchanek and Kerscher, 2007; Nehring, 2011).

A realistic image of humanity would consider aspects like emotions, trust and solidarity, which so far have been left out of the model of *homo economicus*. However, numerous experiments prove the falsity of the assumptions of *homo economicus*. The assumptions must therefore be modified (Suchanek and Kerscher, 2006, p. 60f).

3. Experimental Games

Experimental games offer good possibilities for the representation and derivation of individual behaviour patterns. Although experimental games can cover virtually every situation of social life, any situations where there is an interaction between two or more individuals, of course not all these conditions are worthy of investigation for behavioural economics. In experimental games, behavioural theory approaches that deal with deviations from the economic rational choice model have increasingly been placed in the foreground in recent years, because it was found that the standard economic model could not explain the behaviour in many situations. As a rule, economic researchers deal with the behaviour of individuals in decision situations where a scarce resource is to be divided between two or more persons. This resource can be an asset, a certain amount of money or even a defined number of hours of work. The people involved in the transaction share this resource by negotiating among themselves.

The results of dictator and ultimatum games suggest that the behaviour of people, in addition to selfish motives, is also affected by altruism, fairness and reciprocity (Fehr and Gächter, 2000). In many cases, the actors are not located at the Nash equilibrium;[4] instead the players deviate considerably from rational strategies (Forsythe et al., 1994).

---

[4] Nash equilibrium: "A concept of game theory where the optimal outcome of a game is one where no player has an incentive to deviate from his or her chosen strategy after considering an opponent's choice. Overall, an individual can receive no incremental benefit from changing actions, assuming other players remain constant in their strategies. A game may have multiple Nash equilibria or none at all" (http://www.investopedia.com/terms/n/nash-equilibrium.asp, 02.09.2015).

The extent of deviation varies between studies (Henrich et al., 2004). It is assumed that the presence of social norms is essential for the development of current cooperation.

3.1 Dictator Game

The dictator game is popular and extremely simple (Dufwenberg and Muren, 2006). The dictator game represents a simple form of a sequential game. There is a "dictator" (also called distributor) and a "recipient". The dictator determines how the "cake" is distributed among the two players. The recipient has no right of veto; he is powerless and must accept the offer of the dictator (Eckel and Grossman, 1996).

Because of the impotence of the recipient, the dictator should have a dominant strategy according to which he gives the recipient nothing. However, the theoretical predictions are not observed in the experiments. The offers from the dictators are often greater than 0 (Ockenfels and Raub, 2010). Assuming a utility maximizing "dictator", he would by definition retain the entire amount for himself if he was truly *homo economicus*, and the recipient would get nothing (Camerer, 2003). Initially supported as explanation on standard models of social preferences, which define themselves through as the integration of other persons involved in the transaction on the distribution of material resources. As plausible appear that the conduct of pure altruism is due (Andreoni and Miller 2002). Altruism means thought and action determined by unconditional regard for the welfare of others. Inequality aversion, however, is not associated with emotion. Here the actor draws the greatest benefit from the uniform distribution of a quantity, even though he might need to engage in activities that reduce his material pay-off at the end. The dictator game is rather known as a "one-person-decision game" (Bolton et al., 1998, p. 261).

3.2 Findings

Many clues suggest that the dictator is not motivated solely by his own individual pay-off in the dictator game; that is, the standard theory that "more is better" does not apply.One example is the double-blind dictator game played by **Hoffman et al. (1994)** with 36 dictators. The players could divide a sum of $10. The results looked like this: 65% of participants shared nothing; 20% gave as little as $1; and 10% shared $5. The fairness aspect seems to play a big role in the dictator game (Hoffman, McCabe, Smith, 1996).

If everyone would act according to the concept of *homo economicus*, they would keep the $10 for themselves, but 30% of the participants offer amounts greater than 0. **Eckel and Grossman (1996)** developed the dictator game of Hoffman et al. (1994). They also played a double-blind dictator game. Double-blind means that both sides (experimenter and participants) don´t know each other and the treatment. At first participants were asked to share an amount of $10 among themselves or an outside entity. The results changed in the second round. The readiness to give money to the entity increased massively when the entity was a charitable organization (Eckel and Grossman, 1996). The motivation behind this is "warm glow giving". "Warm glow giving" means that people have a good conscience after they have done something good. This means that they only donate for example in the case that it makes them feel better.

Dufwenberg and Muren (2006) conducted an experiment in which 352 people were able to decide how to allocate 1,000 crowns, knowing the gender of their game partner. It was no double-blind experiment. The participants know one characteristic of the responder. The results were as follows; a) women always received more than men when they were the recipients, and b) women gave more than men when they were dictators (Dufwenberg and Muren, 2006).

Franzen and Pointer (2013) conducted an experiment with 90 participants. The participants played 2 rounds. In the first round people were able to decide how to allocate an amount of 10 €. After the first round, they played again, but in 3-person groups. They had to decide in groups and had an amount of 30 € together. The results looked like this: in the first round participants shared 2.36 € and in the second round they shared 2.42 €. Although they had more money in the second round than in the first, they shared less as their individual decision (Franzen and Pointer, 2013).

The results of the experiments presented here show that we humans are not entirely greedy and purely profit-seeking. It seems more likely that we comply with certain social standards, and our generosity also heavily depends on the attachment to our counterpart. That our giving is not always voluntary, but is motivated by the protection of our external image, can be seen in various studies. Even social pressure plays a role in this context. For our own satisfaction, appropriate behaviour is important and we try to have a kind of moral account that balances "fair" and "unfair". In most laboratory studies, women were a lot more generous than men.

3.3 Criticism of experimental economics

The experimental approach to economic situations enriches the scientific perspective enormously. Nevertheless, some points of criticism should be addressed to allow a further development of the experiments. One such criticism, for example, is that the experiments are always played for money. This assumes the neutrality of money. How would the behaviour of the game player change if it were, for example, played for chocolate, so for goods whose maximum usable quantity is limited?

So many goods have an upper limit beyond which a further accumulation is nonsensical, while for money this limit not yet known. In today's world more money is always better. Other "prices" for participating in these experiments could change the behaviour of the participants and might lead to other findings. Because so far it is unclear whether the orientation of morality is an artefact of the laboratory situation, and because behavioural economists have called for sociological field studies, the "syndicate" experiment brought to light behaviour with real economic activity in its real environment (Henrich et al., 2001, p. 77). What occurs in an economic experiment in a laboratory will not always coincide with what takes place in the real world. In a laboratory, the subjects know they are being watched. A main aspect of economic experiments is finding out if subjects make moral or wealth-maximizing choices. But people are easily influenced if they know they are making decisions in an "artificial environment". It is human nature to act morally if you know you are being watched and judged by an experimenter. In the real world, people are not being watched and therefore will be less inclined to act unselfishly. In addition, experiments can be controlled. Experimenters have the ability to manipulate and make slight changes. Greiner and Ockenfels (2009) noted that theory and laboratory experiments alone are not enough to meet the complexity of real social phenomena in certain contexts. The reason is that models are always abstract reflections of reality. Therefore it is necessary to use case studies and other empirical and theoretical methods as complements to the experiments. Elinor and Ostrom (1990) examined through case studies how communities solve problems; but they did not investigate whether entrepreneur decisions are morally influenced. This was complementary to laboratory tests, because the situation in reality is always multi-dimensional unlike in the experimental conditions of an experiment, which is the weakness of qualitative analysis. Showing whether the existing human tendency to at least partially set aside its own interests also affects real economic activity can only be found "in principle" through field observation. Studies on behavioural economics arrived at a point where the view of the *homo economicus* model is no longer purely negative. It can well be an alternative model, because in both situations, in controlled laboratory experiments as well as in real human actions, people will sacrifice their immediate interests if they trust that the other side will also do so. Similar to behavioural economic experiments and despite all the differences from these, there is the possibility that management may ignore economic interests to a certain extent e.g. in production relocation discussions, at least in the short term, in order to meet the moral demands of the social environment.

4.   Conclusion

The aim of my thesis was to find an answer to the question whether *homo economicus* is alive or not. For this I first described the concept of *homo economicus*, and its properties. As an opposite to the concept of *homo economicus*, I presented in the second part experiments in behavioural science. Therefore I considered different experiments of the dictator game from the literature. I presented the major results of four dictator game experiments. The offers from the dictators are often greater than 0. I then came to the conclusion that experimental and behavioural economics clearly suggest that standard assumptions of *homo economicus* are not completely in accordance with observed human behaviour. Individuals seem to be fairer and less selfish than assumed in almost all important economic theories and models. The explanation is that feelings of fairness, altruism, generosity and trust play a crucial role for the results. Economists have to keep working on incorporating a more realistic human image into their theories, but it is unlikely *homo economicus* will become extinct. The many experiments used to try to prove *homo economicus* actually served to show that in fact not all people act according to the concept.

I also criticised experimental games because, in a laboratory, the subjects know they are being watched and are easily influenced if they know they are making decisions in an "artificial environment". Another point was that the experiments are always played for money. This assumes the neutrality of money. How would the behaviour of the game players change if they played for other things? It is important to look at advantages and disadvantages of both parts. Coase, Olson and Buchanan are some of the authors who applied the assumptions of the economic approach to areas not initially seen as economic areas. The criticism of *homo economicus* centred for decades on the assumption of a rational, self-interested actor who acts with complete information (Frey and Stroebe, 1980, p.83). The assumptions on which it is based were repeatedly refuted and challenged by the theoretical integration of sociological and psychological behavioural assumptions into economic behaviour studies. Actors' preferences are not as consistent and constant as assumed, and information processing is often distorted and flawed, especially when dealing with probabilities and in complex situations. The assumption of rationality in the form of utility maximization as a guiding principle clearly does not correspond to the actual decision-making behaviour, a complex process of adaptation that does not have much in common with coldly calculated optimization (Suchanek 1994). But it was not only the "weak communication" beyond the economic camp that led to misinterpreting *homo economicus*. One has the impression that some of his apologists also forgot his function as a heuristic function, for example when they try to prove that *homo economicus* can be virtuous (Baurman, 1996). The question of whether the behaviour is good or bad is irrelevant and should remain so. With such considerations, the intermingling of the descriptive and normative levels is obvious. And so it should generally be asked to what extent the descriptive view of man, which underpins a theory, is influenced by a normative view (Tietzel, 1981). The most important characteristic of *homo economicus* is his explanatory power, and that is only limited and disputed. Although economists have long known that *homo economicus* lives only in their formulas and models, he has become so familiar that they have come to believe in him. And not entirely without reason: the idea of rationally acting people does not even assume that every single individual behaves so, as required by the models. It is sufficient that the economy in its entirety reacts according to the concept. It is a model for the whole, not for the individual. Not every consumer buys less when prices rise, but on average consumers do spend less. And these movements are the ones which are important to economists.

LITERATURE

Andreoni, J. & Miller, J. (2002): Giving according to GARP: an experimental test of the rationality of altruism. Econometrica

Axel Franzen, Sonja Pointner. Anonymity in the dictator game revisited. Department of Economics and Social Sciences, Institute of Sociology, University of Bern, Lerchenweg 36, 3012 Bern, Switzerland

Bolton, Gary E.; Katok, Elena; Zwick, Rami (1998): Dictator game giving. Rules of fairness versus acts of kindness. In: International Journal of Game Theory 27 (2), S. 269–299

Camerer, Colin F (2003): Behavioral Game Theory – Experiments in Strategic Interaction. New York: Russel Sage Foundation, Princeton University Press.

Dufwenberg, M. & Muren, A. Gender composition in teams. Journal of Economic Behaviour and Organization, 61, 50-54

Eckel, Catherine C.; Grossman, Philip J. (1996): Altruism in Anonymous Dictator Games. In: Games and Economic Behavior 16 (2), S. 181–191.

Fehr, Ernst; Gächter, Simon (2000): Fairness and Retaliation: The Economics of Reciprocity, Journal of Economic Perspectives, 14, Nr. 3, 159 – 181.

Frey, Bruno S.; Stroebe, Wolfgang (1980): Ist das Modell des Homo Oeconomicus 'unpsychologisch'? Zuerich

Hoffman, E., McCabe, K., Shachat, K., & Smith, V.L. (1994): Preferences, property rights, and anonymity in bargaining games. Games and Economic Behavior 7:346-380

Hoffman, E., McCabe, K., & Smith, V. L. (1996): Social distance and other-regarding behavior in dictator games. The American Economic Review, 653-660.

Kirchgässner, Gebhard (1991): Homo oeconomicus – Das ökonomische Modell individuellen Verhaltens und seine Anwendung in den Wirtschafts- und Sozialwissenschaften. Tübingen: Mohr.

Kirchgässner, Gebhard (2008): Homo oeconomicus. Das ökonomische Modell individuellen Verhaltens und seine Anwendung in den Wirtschafts- und Sozialwissenschaften. 3., erg. und erw. Aufl. Tübingen.

Lofthouse, Stephen, John Vint (1978): "Some Conceptions and Misconceptions Concerning Economic Man." Rivista internazionale di scienze economiche e commerciali: 586-615.

Manstetten, R., 2000: Das Menschenbild der Ökonomie. Der homo oeconomicus und die Anthropologie von Adam Smith, Freiburg/München.

Nehring, Martin (2011): Homo oeconomicus. Ein universell geeignetes Modell für die ökonomische Theorie? /Martin Nehring. 1. Aufl. Hamburg

Ockenfels, Axel; Raub, Werner (2010): Rational and Fair. In: Soziologische Theorie kontrovers. Wiesbaden: VS Verl., S. 119–136

Simon, H. A. (1955): A behavioral model of rational choice. *The quarterly journal of economics*, 99-118.

Soukup, Alexandr; Maitah, Mansoor; Svoboda, Roman (2014): The Concept of Rationality in Neoclassical and Behavioural Economic Theory. In: MAS 9 (3).

Suchanek, A., & Kerscher, K. J. (2006): Verdirbt der homo oeconomicus die Moral. Nell, Veronika von/Kufeld, Klaus (Hrsgg.), Homo oeconomicus. Ein neues Leitbild in der globalisierten Welt, 59-79.

Suchanek, A., & Kerscher, K. J. (2007): Der Homo oeconomicus: Verfehltes Menschenbild oder leistungsfähiges Analyseinstrument?. In Individuum und Organisation (pp. 251-275).

Tietzel (1981), Die Rationalitätsannahme in den Wirtschaftswissenschaften,
oder: Der homo oeconomicus und seine Verwandten, in: Jahrbuch für Sozialwissenschaft, Band 32, S. 115-138

Varoufakis, Yanis, and Christian Arnsperger. 2006: What Is Neoclassical Economics? Post-autistic economics review 38 (1).

Online-Resources:

Sciencedaily: www.sciencedaily.com/terms/anchoring.htm, 05.09.2015

Investopedia: www.investopedia.com/terms/n/nash-equilibrium.asp, 02.09.2015

Socialpsychology: http://kahneman.socialpsychology.org/, 05.09.2015